TALKING MASKS

TALKING MASKS

(OEDIPUSSY)

a play by

Adam Seelig

BookThug | Toronto : MMIX

FIRST EDITION
SECOND PRINTING
copyright © Adam Seelig, 2009

The production of this edition was made possible by
BookThug and One Little Goat Theatre Company.

LIBRARY AND ARCHIVES CANADA
CATALOGUING IN PUBLICATION

Seelig, Adam, 1975-   Talking masks : Oedipussy /
Adam Seelig.

A play. ISBN 978-1-897388-39-6

    I. Title.
PS8637.E446 T34 2009   C812'.6   C2009-900583-2

I have made my people somewhat "characterless" for the following reasons. Character must have originally signified the dominating trait of the soul complex, and this was confused with temperament. Later it became a kind of term for the automaton, one whose nature had become fixed or who had adapted himself to a particular role in life. In fact, a person who had ceased to grow was called a character, while one continuing to develop was called characterless, in a derogatory sense, of course, because he or she was so hard to catch, classify, and keep track of. A character came to signify a person fixed and finished.

– August Strindberg

May also be read from the stage

ACT I: PRELUDE

ACT II: FUGUE

ISHMAEL + ISAAC = OEDIPUS

Hagar births Ishmael, Abraham's first; Sarah
has Isaac, his second. Sarah insists Abraham
banish Hagar and son. Ishmael, in exile, makes
a name for himself, founding the Arabs. A *voice*
commands Abraham to bind and sacrifice Isaac on
a mountaintop. Some fear and trembling ensues.
Finally Isaac keeps his life but loses his foreskin –
small price – and thus a covenant is made with
his people, the Jews. His brother, Ishmael, is also

circumcised, as is Father Abraham. (Someone records this.)

Meanwhile...

Oedipus, the original motherfucker, is born. A voice prophesies he'll kill Father and marry Mother, so King Laius and Queen Jocasta bind their baby and leave him for dead on a hilltop. Saved by a shepherd and adopted by a family, baby keeps his life but sustains a lifelong foot injury – small price. A young man now, Oedipus ('wounded feet') runs away from his assumed home. In his hurry he slays an older man on horseback at a crossroads. Later he solves the riddle of the Sphinx (half man, half lion) and is rewarded with a kingship and a recently widowed queen. He's made a name for himself in exile (yes this sounds familiar), until Tiresiass, a shit-disturber, reveals the prophecy came true. Congratulations, Oedipus! Recall the man you killed? Know the woman you married? And Oedipus now recalls. Oedipus now knows. His vision of the past painfully clear, he blinds himself and stumbles off, condemned to remember. (Sophocles writes it all down.)

CAST

Son (**S**)

Man on Horse (**AZ**)

Mother 1 (**M1**)

Mother 2 (**M2**)

STAGE

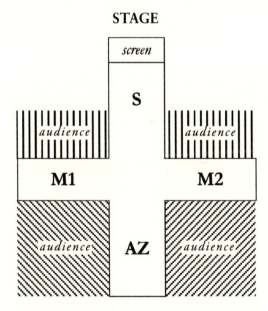

The performers sit and speak into microphones. S's chair should include a 'neck' and 'head' that extend from the chair's 'back/torso'.

If the play is produced in a venue with flexible seating, the audience is seated more or less along the lines drawn. If the stage and seats are fixed, place **S** & **M1** & **M2** on stage and **AZ** on a platform extending from the stage into the audience.

TEXT

There is a screen for textual and photographic projections above and behind **S**. Bold text in the script is projected entirely in capital letters and without punctuation. E.g. **"For the record."** would be projected as **"FOR THE RECORD"** and "You know I could **change you** in **a second, son,** don't you?" could be projected as **"CHANGE YOU A SECOND SON"** or with **"CHANGE YOU"** and **"A SECOND SON"** on separate lines. Most projections will be held on screen for several counts before fading out unless noted otherwise.

Slashes and underlining indicate simultaneous speech, e.g.:

    M2: Don't ever/ be like him.

    M1: <u>Be like him</u>, please.

In some cases simultaneous speech appears on the same line, e.g.:

    M1/M2: Yes/No.

Lines assigned to more than one actor are to be shared or divided by the actors (this mostly applies to **M1 + M2**).

ACT ONE: PRELUDE

While the audience shuffles in project a photo of a horse's rear. A horizontal black bar – the kind that is superimposed, for example, to censor or to preserve anonymity – covers its tail. As the house lights fade to black, project **ASSHOLE** *in the black bar, then fade out the entire projection. Lights up on the faces of* **Son, Mother 1** *and* **Mother 2** *when each says "switch." Their bodies remain unlit. They are seated and speak into microphones.*

s: Switch.

MI + M2: Switch.

Project **A**. *(Note: the following table reads from left to right.)*

S	M1	M2
a a a a	be be be	see see
be be	seen seen seen	da da da da
da da da da	da da da da	
begin	beget	be gone
begin	alone	alone
over again	a grain	a germ
a joke?	affirm	a worm
a term	time	time
to test	test	test
a test	test	atone
for what	belongs	sings
the song	belonging	to think
before you	never think	before you
thing	before you do it	do it
do it	to another	oh brother
my father	closer	farther
away	make	way
for me	my baby	boy
boy	boy	sucks
my thumb	his thumb	his mum
Mama!	baby	Moses
Mama	baby	Mohhamed
Mama	my Isaac	my Ishmael
mama please	my little prince	my little prince
please don't	my little king Oedi- pussy pussy pussy pussy pussy	pussy pussy pussy pussy pussy

don't call me that please	baby	Jesus circum-sised
maybe	baby	drive me crazy
be my dada	don't please	don't mention
abandoned	a bond	and on and on
switch <u>on</u>	<u>on</u>	on
and breathe	life	to end
lies	lie	still
till a theme	gleams	in eye
spy	with my lower-case	i know more than me alone
know more than me	alone know more	than me alone
know more than	me alone know	more than me
alone	know	no more
in threes	<u>please</u>	<u>please</u>
try	another	angle
try	angle	miss
direct	into heart	startle
cock	crows	open
close eyes open	open close	open
head first	<u>coming</u>	<u>coming</u>
son	<u>rising</u>	<u>rising</u>
son	<u>dropping</u>	<u>dropping</u>
son	<u>crowning</u> <u>crowning</u> <u>crowning</u>	<u>crowning</u> <u>crowning</u> <u>crowning</u>
now	<u>switchhhhhh...</u>	<u>switchhhhhh...</u>

Lights fade out. M1 + M2 exit in the dark while the sound of their "shhhhhhhhhhh…", recorded, continues to emanate from loudspeakers.

*Project **PRELUDE**. Lights up on all of S, causing him to squint. Sitting on a chair, he is wearing a large diaper with a zipper. His ankles are bound by a strap attached to his chair.*

S (*straining to see the surroundings*): Hello. Hello?

*Lights up on **Man on Horse (AZ)**, across from S. He sits on a coin-operated horse and is wearing a thin, black, Zorro-like mask. He is mounted backwards on the horse so that he and the horse's rear face S. Project and hold a photo of **AZ**'s masked face.*

AZ: Hey.

S (*making an effort to see **AZ***): Hey. (*Pause.*)

AZ: Neigh.

S: Neigh?

AZ (*neighing*): Neigh.

S: Is that a horse?

AZ: Yeah, a stallion, but I just spoke for him. He

only performs for money.

S: What's he called?

AZ: **What's his name?** (*Project the words in a black bar that covers AZ's mask and eyes in the photo, then fade out the photo and hold the words.*) I call him Master, Master Thespian. (*AZ takes a coin out of his pocket.*) Listen. (*Inserts it into the horse's coin box.*)

AZ's *voice* (*recorded, his neighing voice emanates from a speaker in the horse's rear.*): Neigh.

S: Here Master Master Master... (*He gets up and attempts to walk towards the horse only to discover his ankles are bound. Off microphone, acoustically.*) Shit. (*Sits back down. Resumes speaking into microphone.*) Are you there?

AZ (*lifts mask onto forehead*): **For the record** I am.

S: I can't see clearly.

AZ: You will, gradually.

S: Like what?

AZ: A blur, a breast, your mother's different faces, then your own your own your own until nothing.

S: You mean blind.

AZ: It could happen in **a second, son**.

S: Son? (*Pause.*) You are here, aren't you?

AZ: Shall we? (*Lights start dimming on S.*)

S: Already? (*Lights stop dimming, then fade back up.*) Thank you. (*Pause.*) I'm sure my hearing's fine. Say something else. (*Pause.*)

AZ: I'm sorry.

S: Why?

AZ: No, I didn't mean to apologize – that was my Canadian propriety talking – what I meant is that I'd prefer not to engage in mindless chit chat because with The Master here everything ends up being for the record.

S: For the record, meaning…?

AZ: You're **being recorded**.

S: Now? Now? (*AZ takes out another coin from his pocket and inserts it into the horse's coin box.*)

S's voice (*from the horse*): Now? Now?

AZ: You're your own big **brother**.

S: But it's just me.

AZ: **Double you**.

S: I'm still free to say –

AZ: Free as you're bound. Look down again.

S: Then I'm a tree.

AZ: **You're a boy**.

S: I'm a tree.

AZ: **Don't be precious, be** –

S: Fine, I'm *like* a tree.

AZ: No **metaphors** or **similes**, please.

S: A tree falling in the middle of –

AZ: Or platitudes. **Direct speech**.

S: How much more direct could I be?

AZ: You could be **prompter**.

S: Prompt my ass.

AZ: I'll have it smacked if you keep that up. You
obviously need a change.

S (*indicating diaper*): I'm okay for now in this one.

AZ: Then before this degenerates any further...
(*Lights start dimming on S.*)

S: No, wait! (*Lights stop dimming.*)

AZ: You know I could **change you** in **a second, son,**
don't you?

S: Please don't –

AZ: Don't you? (*Pause.*)

S: Maybe. (*Lights fade back up on S.*)

AZ: **There are others.**

S: Like you?

AZ: **Like you.**

S: So you want just another Tom, a Dick, a Norm.

AZ: It keeps the record clean.

S: But prevents me from saying –

AZ: Just remember you're **nothing without others.**

S: Listen: I – don't – need – you.

AZ: Interesting. Go ahead, Master. (*Inserts a coin
into the coin box.*)

S's *voice (from the horse)*: **I – need – you.**

S: You perverted what I said.

AZ: Converted it, into **sound bites, meaning.**

S: But…

AZ: You can still talk to us.

S: What for, if you're just going to – ?

AZ: For a **sense of brotherhood.** Anyway, **you can't leave** yet.

S: Who made you king?

AZ: **Stop being a child.**

S: Then I'll be a baby.

AZ: You'll have to come **out of the light,** son, eventually. (*Lights start dimming on* **S**.)

S: Wait. (*Lights stop dimming.*) **Cut the son** bullshit, would you. (*Hold.*)

AZ: I see what's on your mind.

S: What?

AZ: Cut… Just like your **brother,** and your **father.**

(*Replace* **SON** *in previous projection with* **BROTHER,** *then* **FATHER.**)

S: What do you mean? (*Lights back up.*)

AZ: That's how you **become a man,** by **following the path** before you.

S: Do you need to be so cryptic? Let's just have a simple conversation, just talk.

AZ: **In beautiful clichés?**

S: If that's what it takes. Like… what's your sign?

AZ: You're not serious.

S: What's your sign? (*Pause.*)

AZ: I'm a Leo, okay.

S. A Leo, I wouldn't have guessed.

AZ: Then **figure** it out later **by yourself.**

S: When I'm wanking in the dark?

AZ: **Doing what in the dark?**

S: Wanking. Masturbating. Don't tell me you don't do it.

AZ: Of course I do. **Letting yourself go**…

S (*laughs*): "Letting yourself go."

AZ: That's **enough, young man**.

S: Why be such a prude about it? Let me guess· I'll
go blind.

AZ: I'm trying to keep you from –

S (*starts unzipping fly*): Never seen a private part
before?

AZ: **Stop this right now**, please, for the record, son,
I mean, uh, what's-your-name… I need to call you
something. Is Ben okay, son?

S: Anything but son.

AZ: Okay listen, Ben, dear dear Ben, there's no
reason to be crass. I'm perfectly familiar with
private parts, so keep it in your diaper please.

S: For the sake of your Canadian etiquette, I
suppose.

AZ: I'm American too, so don't get carried away.

S: You're American?

AZ: Nobody's perfect. I'm also German.

S: Now you're making it up.

AZ: No really, I'm German.

S: How?

AZ: My father.

S: Where's he from, Munich?

AZ: Israel, actually.

S: So you're a Jew.

AZ: Not necessarily.

S: You just said your father's Israeli.

AZ: He could be an Arab, I mean a non-Jewish
    Arab.

S: Is he circumcised? Are you circumcised?

AZ: Mind your own.

S: Do you eat pork?

AZ: I'd love to.

S: But you don't.

AZ: That could make me a Muslim.

S: You don't look Muslim.

AZ: And how's that?

S: You don't fit the profile.

AZ: What about now? (*AZ turns his head to one side. Project a facial profile of AZ wearing Groucho Marx joke glasses.*)

S: Jew.

AZ: And now? (*AZ turns his head. Project AZ's other profile in the same glasses.*)

S: Total Jew. (*Project the photo of AZ's masked face from earlier and hold.*) Admit it, your father is a Jew, your mother is a Jew, and you're a Jew.

AZ (*puts mask back on*): Piss off.

S: You can say it: my father is a Jew, my mother is a Jew, and I'm a Jew.

AZ: That's interesting...

S: What is?

AZ: Let's go, Master Thespian.

S: You're going?!

AZ: I have enough material for the record now.

S: Like what?

AZ: Don't tell him, Master. Let's go. (*Starts to turn around on the horse.*)

S: Why are you avoiding me?

AZ (*faces S and lifts mask onto forehead*): I don't need this interrogation, Ben. What are you trying to extort, and what for?

S: I just want to know the facts.

AZ: To use them against me.

S: There's nothing to be ashamed of.

AZ: But all this personal horseshit can't be struck from the record, Ben. Even if at first it's not **apparent,** we're stuck with it, and your mother will be too. (*Project **A PARENT**.*)

S: My mother... Is she here?

AZ: She will be.

S: What about my father? (*Pause.*)

AZ: We better leave it at that, Ben.

S: Will he be here too?

AZ: Let's say... he'll be out of sight, okay?

S: Watching me?

AZ: Or...

S: Listening? (*Pause.*) Or... what? Or what?

AZ: I can't say, Ben.

S: Dead?

AZ: Not...

S: Not necessarily dead.

AZ: I can't say, son.

S: Ben.

AZ: I'm sorry, Ben, I can't say.

S: Should I say something then?

AZ: What for?

S: Just in case.

AZ: In case he's dead or in case he's alive?

S: Either way.

AZ: What's there to say?

S: A prayer, maybe.

AZ: A prayer? (*Chuckles.*) You might want to zip up your fly first.

S: What's your problem with nudity?

AZ: It's not the nudity so much as your being uncircumcised. (*S looks under his diaper to inspect.*) If you're already reciting a prayer you should at least do it right.

S: Who says I'm Jewish?

AZ: Or Muslim?

S: Or Muslim, who says?

AZ: Your birth.

S: So I have to be…?

AZ: Circumcised.

S: No! What?! (*Pause.*) Why?

AZ: No reason was ever given to Abraham. (*Project and hold FATHER ABRAHAM.*)

S: This is barbaric.

AZ: No, it's tribal, and you should save your breath because it's your mothers who will ultimately conduct it, not me.

S: My mothers, plural?

AZ: Mother, mothers, **maybe one, maybe two**. What's important is that you hide what you've got while you've still got it.

S (*zips fly*): There, done.

AZ: Then go ahead, pray away if you want.

S (*hesitates*): I don't know what to say.

AZ: Make it up.

S (*hesitates again*): Do you think you could help me?

AZ: All you have to do is put your hands together like this... (**AZ *puts his palms together in front of his chest and S emulates this 'prayer' pose.***) Bow your head... (*S does so.*) That's it. Now just sit like that for a few moments and you're done.

S (*looks up*): But what should I say?

AZ: Nothing, Ben, whatever you want. As long as you hold that pose it really doesn't matter

if you're thinking "oh father oh father etc."
At least for the record it doesn't. So, get into
position. (*S does so.*) Good. We can even
provide some accompanying music to make it
feel more authentic. (*Inserts a coin into the coin
box. Emanating from the horse, the alarming
beginning of Penderecki's "Threnody for the
Victims of Hiroshima" startles both of them.*)
What the – ?! Where the hell did that come from,
Master? (*AZ bangs on the horse, causing the
music to change suddenly to an instrumental
version of "Father Abraham," the children's folk
song. It should sound tinkly and childlike – like
most amusement rides – while at the same time,
oddly liturgical.*) There, that's more like it. (*To S.*)
Go ahead. (*S resumes 'prayer' pose.*)

The music eventually ends. S stops 'praying.'

AZ: What were you thinking about?

S: My father.

AZ: You remembered him?

S: I tried.

AZ: In vain, so you thought about yourself, right?
(*Pause.*) It's okay to be a little self-involved, Ben.
You said the prayer for yourself.

S: Well…

AZ: Didn't you, Ben. Maybe you even "imagined your own funeral," mourned a little for your future dead self, a silent prayer for the Ben we all once knew and loved?

S: Maybe.

AZ: Good. So did I. Now… (*Lights start dimming on S.*)

S: Wait. (*Lights stop dimming.*) Who did you mourn for? You?

AZ: You. (*Project **W**.*)

S: Me? That's absurd. I'm not dead. (*Pause.*) Hello. Hello? I'm not dead.

AZ: You will be.

S: But so will everyone, eventually.

AZ: Except in your case.

S: In my case… what?

AZ: We know when. (*Pause.*)

S: You've got to be…!

AZ: No. We know when you'll die.

S: Will you tell me?

AZ: You sure you want to know?

S: Of course I want to know! (*Lights fade back up on S.*)

AZ: Alright, Master, let him hear it. (*Takes a coin out of pocket.*) Right after this. (*Inserts the coin into the coin box. Nothing happens.*) **Come on**, Master! (*Inserts another coin. Nothing. He grabs the reins and flogs the horse repeatedly.*) Come on, Thespian, play it!!

S: Whoa, hold on.

AZ: Shh. I think it's coming.

M1 + M2's *voices* (*from the horse*): Switch.

AZ: That's it.

M1 + M2's *voices* (*from loudspeakers*): Switch.

S: Okay… great… and when exactly will that happen?

AZ: In about an hour.

S: An hour?! That's nothing!

AZ: Depends on your perspective.

S: But don't you want me to live?

AZ: Of course, but only up to a point.

S: Why?

AZ: Ah, why again. And again, Ben, there's no reason, I hate to say. With birth we can usually figure out why – a woman loves or, God forbid, she's raped – but death? Unless you're deliberately killed or you deliberately kill yourself, there's no intention behind it, just time: 81 years, 81 months, 81 minutes. Wait, did I seriously just hear myself say "God forbid"? God forbid. I've got to **purge** these ridiculous phrases from my system. Listen, don't be misled by the purposeful and moral endings of all those great tragedies: you're not evil, greedy, deluded, fatally flawed. You simply act against the clock until your time is up like all of us. We are your fate and your frame just as time is ours, and I'm telling you this frame can sit on its ass and watch for only so long. Isn't that right, Master? Two hours tops. Now... (*Lights start dimming on S.*)

S: Just one more question. Please! (*Dimming stops.*) How? I know when, thank you, I guess, but *how*, please, how will it... how will I end?

AZ: You'll forget all this later anyway, Ben. Maybe a part of what I say will remain with you, a remembered remnant of some sort, but mostly you'll forget. "To **forget** is to remember without pain." Have you heard that one?

S: To forget… (*Lights fade back up on S.*)

AZ: Yeah. "To **forget** is to remember without pain." But to have pain is to be born again. You'll see later on.

S: Will you still be here?

AZ: Yes, but out of sight.

S: Watching?

AZ: And listening, because what you'll say, while new to you, will cover what we've just said, just as what we're saying now lies on top of what was covered before, which also lies –

S: Okay okay, fine. Now will you please tell me how it will happen? Please.

AZ: With the bad breath of history in every word.

S: I'm asking about my end, my *death*, and all I get is another riddle?!

AZ: Look, there's more to all this than you, Ben. You're not some virgin birth, some miraculous dawning of time, some immaculate *tabula rasa*, because your mothers loved a thousand ways to birth you after others and among others meaning more than you knew with your words lying not as the ciphering dummy of a ventriloquist but in search of an absent truth we know is there, the real concealed multilayered shit archaeologists thrust their hands into while we dig no deeper than our nostrils – so no, Ben, I'm not speaking in riddles, and if, if, then they're riddles of the sphincter full of the stuff that makes us after all. You're not an archetype and you're not an original because **in the beginning** it was Abraham who made you, Sarah who birthed you, Hagar who shaped you, Sophocles who wrote you. (*Hold.*) No, what you are is an individual recovered by your mother's **bare sheet**. (*Add.*)

M1's *voice*: Bare sheet.

M2's *voice*: Bare sheet.

AZ: The **rest** will follow. (*Add.*)

S: But you never answered the question. What about – ?

AZ: Your beginning, your end? Either you'll forget or you'll be born again. (*Takes a coin out of pocket.*) I have what I need for the record, Ben, so let's move on this time, please, **in peace**.

*The entire projection now reads: **IN THE BEGINNING / BARE SHEET / REST IN***

PEACE. *AZ blindfolds himself with the mask – i.e. wears it backwards, the eye-holes now at the back of his head.*

AZ: Here we go, Master Thespian.

> *AZ drops the coin into the horse and we hear S's recorded voice playing in a continuous loop.*

S's *voice (from the horse)*: My father is a Jew, my mother is a Jew, and I'm a Jew. My father is a Jew, my mother is a Jew, and I'm a Jew. My father is a Jew……

> *AZ turns around to face forwards on the horse and away from S.*

AZ (*acoustically, off microphone*): Giddyup!

> *The horse is set in motion as the sound loop of S's voice spreads to all the loudspeakers. S strains to see AZ 'ride off'. The lights fade out on S, who senses them going down, and a Zorro-like 'Z' is projected.*

*Project the following equation continuously
in both directions, cross-fading between each
element:*

OEDIPUS = ISAAC + ISHMAEL

House lights to black. Project **FUGUE.**

AZ's *voice*: When ready to perform the act, the
parents take their infant and joyously proclaim...

*We hear the beginning of a prayer chanted
in Hebrew: "Baruch ata Hashem Eloheinu
melech ha'olam asher kidshanu bemitzvotav
vetzivanu..."*

AZ's *voice*: ...blessed are you, The Name, our God,
king of the universe, who has sanctified us and
commanded us to –

M1 + M2's *voices*: **Cut!**

> *Hold projection. After a few beats add* **THE SON** *to create* **CUT THE SON**, *then replace* **SON** *with* **BROTHER**, *then* **BROTHER** *with* **FATHER**.
> *Lights up gradually on the faces of* **M1 + M2** *during the following section. Working with vocal and audio effects, echoes, etc., they draw on only two words each to create various permutations and a broad soundscape:*

{ **M1**: yes...... and......

{ **M2**: no...... but......

> *Etc., ending with:*

M1: Yes. (*Long pause.*)

M2: Yes. (*Pause.*)

> *Project* **PURGE** *and hold throughout the following 'alphabetical' section until the last letter is projected. Lights up on S's face.*

S: One.

M1: Two.

M2: Three.

M1 + M2: For the record
    tethered
    we

S: we-we

M1 + M2: free yet
    tied together
    in one un-
    conscious son says

S: **A B**

M1 + M2: and me me me (*Project* **C**.)
    a name
    I call my
    fa fa fa
    so so so
    alive with the sound of

S: **D**. (*Lights up on* **AZ**'*s microphone. The horse and* **AZ** *are gone.*)

M1 + M2: Can you say…?

S: Daaaa…

M1 + M2: Almost.

S: Daaaa…

M1 + M2: Good.

S: Dada. (*Lights out on AZ's microphone.*)

M1 + M2: Alright dada for example (*Project E G, hold.*)
  and for example for example and
  Forgetting (*Add F to the middle of the held projection above.*)
  the first thing you heard when you were born.

> *We hear the beginning of a prayer chanted in Arabic: "Allahu Akbar. Allahu Akbar."*

M1 + M2: Do you remember?

S: I forget. (*Drop E and G, leaving only F projected.*)

M1 + M2: You forgot that?
  Forgot that/ feeling

S: <u>Feeling</u> Horny

M1 + M2 + S: oh yes
  give it to me
  give me an/ H
  <u>H</u> for
  hhhhhhhhhhhhhhhheart
  Involuntarily
  in vol vol vol vol
  flying a Jew is a Kite on the mike is a victim
  you're sure
  Lamenting Me Now now now now now...
  O o o o o ...

M1: Please

M2: don't

M1 + M2 + S: Question Remembrance Sings past
Tomorrow

M2: and tomorrow

M1: I love

M2: and tomorrow

M1: you're only/ a

M2: a way of recording/ time

S: time

M1: my little orphan

S: time you (*U*) View two other yous (**W**)

M1 + M2 + S: double
X
whY congratulations (*Hold XY.*)
you're the mother of a
chromosomic
chronosonic
technotronic
hooked on phonic

S: What? I'm a boy.

M1 + M2: He's a boy?

S: But my parents won't admit it.

M1 + M2: He's a goy.

S: I'm a who?

M1 + M2: Until your circum –
  Bris for the record it's a *bris*. Circumcision sounds
    so…
  Listen.

  > *Briefly excerpt the Hebrew prayer again:*
  > *"Baruch ata Hashem…"*

  It's your/ you know
  <u>you know</u> the ritual
  the covenant of what's-his-name.

S: Will it hurt?

M1 + M2: To pee?

S: To please you.

M1: Peace will be with you, my son, *shalom*

M2: *salaam*

S: salami salami

M1: Salome/ Salome

M2: <u>Salome</u> always gets ahead of her man

M1: a piece of her boy

S: Why? (*Drop* X, *leaving only* Y *projected.*)

M2: For father

M1: To open

M2: the gates of

M1: the head of

M2: a piece of

M1: the lions

M2: the gates of

M1: the for of

M2: the skin of

M1: the skin of

M2: the mask of

M1 + M2: Zzzzzzzzion.

A Zorro-like 'Z' is projected and the stage goes to black. Pause.
Lights up on all of M1, and dimly up on the audience. Project MASKque. In the following 'character exposition' actors fill in the blanks according to their true biography and call each other, except for S, by their actual names.

M1 (*to audience*): My name is _(M1)_ . I'm a mother. If I wear a mask it shows. I was born in _____ and I live in _____. I enjoy late-night movies, long walks on the beach and acting, and my pet peeves are pushy people, dirty diapers and alliteration. I hope this description covers me. _(M2)_ ? (*Lights up on all of M2.*)

M2 (*to audience*): Thanks, _(M1)_ . My name is _(M2)_ . I'm another mother. If I wear a mask it shows variety. I was born in _____ but I live in _____. I enjoy playing for real while my pet peeves are other people's vices, my own devices and the perfect hermetic closure of rhyming couplets despite my occasional admiration for linguistic virtuosity in the theatre. In the end the play's the thing wherein I – . Nevermind. I feel some desire from you, maybe even love, but won't be fooled into opening my centre folded and tucked away in that special place you know so well when you fuck yourself. Go. That is all you need to know. Limit truth to beauty and beauty

to truth if you want to be romantic, just don't
reduce me to some cheap character revealing the
cleavage between her past and present through
nauseatingly poignant personal details. I will be
and act but not pretend. That's why what I say
protects me from, you know, the public, infection.
Still, thank you for coming. _(M1)_ ?

M1: It's his turn now.

> *House lights out. Stage lights up on all of S.*
> *He is clothed but shoeless. His ankles and bare*
> *feet are no longer bound, and there is no sign*
> *of the strap that previously bound them.*

S (*unaware of audience*): My name is to be
determined. I'm more than just another
motherfucker. (**M1 + M2** *laugh.*) I enjoy catching
conscience and cupping conches when it's my
turn to speak on the sand mother plays on. I was
born in _____ and I live in _____. I'm running
away, I feel, from feeling? Maybe. Somewhere
else? Could be. Becoming something or other
in the future I don't know, but I resent – okay,
call it a pet peeve – my pet peeve is being called
names...

M1: My little Y.

M2: You little X.

S: ...when I should be the Lord of (feeling his

crotch)… my fly's undone. (*M1 + M2 laugh. S zips his fly.*) Very funny.

M1 + M2: Oh Isaac. (*Project and hold a photo of S's face.*)

S: Don't call me that please for the record too much in view makes me shudder out damn light spots innocent under view of you like to watch the news don't you catch my love looking you look at me drift to ward words branch and thin branch thinner than once I was one fat trunk before branching into specifici-fici-fici-fici –

M2: Specificity. (*Project and hold a facial profile of S.*)

M1: Well said, dear.

S: Specificity for two words make three meanings branch artifici-fici-fici-fici –

M2: Artificial.

M1: Well said, love. (*Project and hold S's other profile.*)

S: Artificial cages thin body lessened taught age old know how tongue forks the record may track some but you couldn't you can't you won't catch my first fat *aeiouyyyyyyyyyy*!!!

M2: Oh my, what on earth do you mean?

S: *Aeiouyyyyyyyyyy*, approximately. (*Project and hold S's face again.*)

M1: Well I can't understand when you speak so.

M2: Wild.

S: Yes please thank you very no I'd prefer to excuse me *s'il vous plaît*. (*Fade out projection.*)

M1 + M2: Bravo! That's my baby. What a good boy. Much/ better.

S: <u>Better</u> hide my hide behind word curtain draws mental manners cages masks runts grunt bye-bye tree leaves apple please mind your poos and pees hide that hard on first sin drafts through curtain crack cold cage lessens flesh tongue plays record back needling blood past member can't forget apple leaves tree in me man I could end better without curtain letting blood fork tongue lie words into cunning lips apart slip in deep fork pleases wounds mother forking snakes and letters wounds pleases wounds pleases wounds and goes in for the still man's first word is woman, woman's is/ please.

M1 + M2: <u>Please</u>!

M1: Oh

M2: No

S: I said too much.

M1 + M2: I haven't said enough **for the record**.
   (*Pause.*)

S: Why do I feel like I'm missing something?

M2 (*to M1*): Can you handle this one?

S: Mom?

M1 (*to S*): Well because

M2: you see

M1: a tree

M2: understand

M1: leaves an apple which

M2: do you follow?

M1: leaves a tree.

M2: That's you.

S: Then I fall.

M1 + M2: Not far.

S: But what have I done?

M1 + M2: You were born
in a word wanting
another mother brother father
a parent
more. (*Pause.*)

S: I need to make a wee-wee. (*S relieves himself in his pants.*)

M1 + M2: That's okay.

S: I don't feel okay.

M1 + M2: Then I'll **change you**. (*Hold.*)

S: Please don't.

M2: But you're dirty.

M1: You'll feel better in **a second, son,** once I change you. (*Add.*)

S: Please don't.

M1 + M2: In a second, son...

S: I'm clean.

M1 + M2: ...you'll feel better.

S: I swear.

M1 + M2: You see, you're dirty dirty/ dirty.
<u>Dirty</u>.
In a second son you'll feel –

S: Stop with the second son, second son, second son.
(*Pause. Hold only **A SECOND SON**.*) What?
What, Mom?

M2 (*to M1*): You tell him.

M1: Me again, why?

M2: I'll help you.

S: What, Mom, what, what, what, what, what, what,
what, what, what......? (*S continues this under
M1 + M2 until his next line.*)

M1 (*To M2*): If he'd just shut up for a second I
could think of what to say. They're unbelievable,
aren't they?

M2: You're telling me. No patience.

M1: Makes you want to... Makes you want to...

M2: Makes you want to shake them, doesn't it.

S: Mom? (*Pause.*) Mom?

M1 (*sighs*): It's true, son. You have a –

M2: Had a.

M1: You tell him then!

M2: You're doing fine.

S: I have a – ?

M2: *Had* a...

M1: *Had*, I mean yes, you had a.

S: A what?

M1: An older **brother**. (*Pause.*)

S: I...

M2: You did.

M1: There are two of you.

M2: *Were*, there *were*. You'll mislead him. You can't let him believe.

M1: I mean there *were* two of you. A bond.

M2: Abandoned.

M1: **Double you.**

M2: Half.

M1: **Following the path** before you.

M2: **In beautiful clichés.**

M1: For the record.

S: Why didn't you tell me?

M1: It's **prompter,** cleaner this way. Now let's change you.

M2: Switch.

S: Please don't.

M2: Just like your brother.

M1: He never changed.

M2: W. (*Project and hold ISHMAEL.*)

M1: W. My first.

S: And my…?

M2: Only half brother, but…

M1: And…

S: Then…

M1/M2: And then/But then…

S: Well?

M2: No…

M1: Yes…

M1/M2: and/but…

S: Say it!

M2: Don't ever/ be like him.

M1: <u>Be like him</u>, please.

S: I'll try, I guess.

M1 + M2: God bless.

S: I guess.

M1: Just don't leave.

M2: He deserved it.

M1 (*indicating M2*): She made him go!

M2 (*to S*): That little shit was mocking you.

M1: He was a child!

M2: In the beginning maybe, but –

M1: A child, for God's sake.

M2: But for the record. Don't worry…

M1: How can I not?

M2: …he'll still make a name for himself.

M1: And what about what you ought

M2: not

M1: you ought

M2: not

M1: you ought

M2: not

M1: you ought

M2: not

M1: thou shalt

M2: not

M1: and **sound bites meaning** and –

S: Mom! You're confusing me.

M1 + M2: I am?

M1: You'll **figure** it out later, son.

M2: **By yourself.**

M1: **Doing what in the dark.**

S: Doing what in the dark?

M1 + M2: **Letting yourself go.**

M2: **Out of the light,** son. (*Hold.*)

S: What do you mean?

M1: Out of the sunlight.

S: What do you mean "letting myself go"?

M1/M2: Yes/No.

S: And doing what by myself?

M1/M2: Yes/No.

S: *To* myself?

M1/M2: Yes/No.

S: Is it me you're talking about?

M1/M2: Yes/No.

S: Or my brother?

M1/M2: Yes/No.

S: Father?

M1/M2: Yes/No.

S: Enough riddles!

M1/M2: Yes/No.

S: Is it me my brother or father?!

M1/M2: Yes/No, Yes/No, Yes/No...

> *This reverberates and accumulates. Fade out
> lights on S and fade out projection.*

M1: He made me more/ your father

M2: <u>your father</u> made me

M1: switch

M2: off how to switch off how he made me

M1: a mother

M2: made me

M1: queen

M2: **bare**

M1: more

M2: lift my **sheet** (*Hold **BARE SHEET**.*)

M1: naked

M2: made me make

M1: love

M2: lay you down

M1: tickle tickle

M2: leave you for dead

M1: switch

M2: off how to switch off

M1: love

M2: here we go again

M1: love

M2: for fuck's sake

M1: oh

M2: no

M1 + M2: so this is what it is to

M1: oh

M2: no

M1 + M2: so this is what it is to

M1: oh

M2: no

M1 + M2: so this is what –

M1: more yes

M2: no

M1 + M2: maybe sewn seeds

M2: he was more than me

M1: I

M2: nameless faceless

M1: I can't/ stop

M2: <u>stop</u>

M1: don't/ stop

M2: <u>stop</u> this.

M1: **In the beginning** I was blank, a voice (*Add.*)

M2: avoiding.

S'*s voice*: Hello. Hello?

M1 + M2: There you are
    in the beginning trying to see a… a…
    a body knowing a… a…
    a bare sheet/ no
    <u>no</u>body knows/ tomorrow
    <u>tomorrow</u> thinks of/ you
    <u>you</u> grow you breathe

M1: from naked beginning to

M2: make it end (*Fade out projection.*)

M1: again/ please

M2: <u>please</u> stop

M1: I can't/ stop

M2: <u>stop</u>

M1: you can't/ stop

M2: <u>stop</u>

M1: you don't/ stop

M2: <u>Stop</u>!

> *In the following lines **M1**'s rhythm remains constant while **M2** provides varying syncopations. As an example here, **M1** speaks the full text while **M2** utters the underlined words only.*

M1 + M2: <u>Don't</u> stop don't <u>stop</u> don't stop <u>don't</u> stop don't <u>stop</u> don't stop <u>don't</u> stop don't <u>stop</u> don't stop <u>don't</u> stop don't <u>stop</u> don't stop……

> *Etc.. Together they build and crescendo, ending with:*

M1 + M2: STOP!!! (*Pause as they catch their breath.*)

M1 (*to **M2***): I was you for a moment.

M2 (*to **M1***): For a moment I was your double, you./ Switch.

M1: <u>Switch</u>.

Lights up on **S.**

S: Hello?

M1 + M2: Son!

S: Hello.

M1 + M2: I love you. Won't you tell me?

S: I love you.

M1 + M2: Awww.

S: I love you.

M1 + M2: I love you too.

S: I love you, Mother.

AZ's *voice* + **M1** + **M2**: That's **enough, young man**.
   (*Hold.*)

S: I think I heard… Did you – ?

M2: No.

S: Because I thought that I heard.

M1: That was –

M2: No one. It was nothing. (*Takes a breath.*)

Now let's begin. (*Project and hold* **IN THE BEGINNING**.)

S: A.

M1 + M2: Good.

S: B.

M1 + M2: Good.

S: Begat.

M1 + M2: Then...

S: Be scattered.

M1 + M2: Then...

S: Besot, sought.

M1 + M2: Then...

S: Bereft, reft, reft.

M1 + M2: Then let there/ be...

S: <u>Be</u> light, light, light.

M1 + M2: And so...

S: See reft and light...

M1 + M2: Yes.

S: ...light from reft...

M1 + M2: Yes.

S: ...reft from sought...

M1 + M2: Yes.

S: ...sought from scatter and scatter from gat begat begot in the beginning. (*Fade out projection.*)

M1 + M2: Very good!
Now over
again

S: Repeat, repeteat teat, repetit tit tit.

M1 + M2 (*to each other*): Is he...?

S: Repeteethhhhhhhhhhhh! (*Biting his tongue at the end of the word.*)

M1 + M2 (*clutch breasts*): Ow
don't bite
that hurts Mama.

S: Could I have a taste?

M1: Honey...

S: Just a little bit of milk.

M2: Honey...

S: A teeny tiny taste.

M1 + M2: You're weaned.

S: Then can I have a horsy?

M1 (*to M2*): Where did that come from?

M2 (*to M1*): No idea.

S: Please.

M1: Now son, I love you –

M2: But...

S: Just a teeny tiny horse.

M2: Don't be silly. Aren't I enough? You have me.

M1: And yourself, you can play with yourself.

S: How? (*Pause.*) How, Mom?

M2 (*to M1*): Psst.

M1: What?

M2: You don't mean he should get to know his... his what's-it-called.

M1: Oh. (*Chuckles.*) God no!

S: How, Mom, how?

M1 + M2: Hold on, son, I'm thinking.

M1 (*to M2*): I can't believe you called it his what's-it-called! Why be such a prude? Let me guess, if he plays with it, he'll go blind! (*Laughs.*) We can't keep him from discovering himself.

M2: We can try to put it off.

S: How Mom how Mom how? (*Pause.*)

M2: Say something.

M1: It's a good question, son. Well, make-believe, that's one way to play with yourself. (*M2 clears her throat to correct M1.*) I mean play on your own.

S: Alone?

M2: No, not like him.

M1: I'd never let you go.

S: What if you did?

M1: And strike you from the record?

S: What if?

M1 + M2: Now Isaac…

S: Don't call me –

M1 + M2: Isaac…

S: Don't/ call –

M1 + M2: *Calm* down, my little

M1: metaphor

M2: simile.

S: Use my real name, *Mom*.

M1 + M2: Now Isaac, for the record thou shalt –

S: No, not for the record, not Isaac! My name as it is, *(M1)* , *(M2)* . You know my name. *(M1)* ? *(M2)* ?

M1 + M2: Dear Isaac.

S: Don't.

M1 + M2: Innocent Isaac.

S: Stop.

M2: But you're **being recorded**.

S: By?

M1 + M2: You know.

M1 + M2: **You're a boy**.

S: Thank you for the insight.

M1 + M2: **A sense of brotherhood**.

S: You don't sound like yourself.

M1 + M2: **Like you**.

S: Are you okay?

M1 + M2: **Don't be precious, be**.

S: Be like him, don't be. Thou shalt, thou shalt not. Will you make up your mind?

M1 + M2: **There are others**.

S: Now I'm completely lost.

M1 + M2: **Stop being a child**.

S: Are you even listening, *(M1)* ?

M1 + M2: Direct speech.

S: _(M2)_ ?

M1 + M2: Direct speech.

S: Then speak for yourself. I'm going.

M1 + M2: What?!

S: I'm going.

M1 + M2: You can't leave.

S: Why not?

M1: Because…

M2: Because…

M1 + M2: …I need…

M1: …**you.** (_Project and hold **I NEED YOU**._)

M2: …you. (_Project and hold **I NEED DOUBLE YOU**._)

S: So much for love. Just let me go.

M2: I can't, son.

M1: You're part of me.

M2: We're tied.

S: Exactly, and I can't be anymore, so seriously,
  (M1) , (M2) –

M1: Now/ Isaac.

M2: Isaac, really.

S: Stop branding me.

M1 + M2: Branding?/ I'm blessing you.
  I'm blessing you to multiply.
  My only son.

S: There were two of us, Mom.

M2: Maybe one.

M1: Maybe two.

S: I had a brother. You said so yourself. Why are you changing the story?

M1 + M2: *You're* my son.

S: So was/ he.

M1 + M2: He had to go.

S: You made him.

M1: I made/ you…

M2: <u>You</u> little shit.

M1: …and with God as my witness…

S: Oh God.

M1: …I have chosen you.

S: To be your only son? It's a lie. I have a –

M2: Had.

S: Have, had, who knows, do you? For all we know he's still alive. I have a brother.

M1 + M2: A half brother.
Double you.

S: Whatever he is.

M1 + M2: Was.

S: This is horseshit. I'm going.

M1 + M2: Fine.
Make a mistake.
Get lost.
Wander.

Go.
Fuck yourself for all I care.
Become a man.

S: Stop avoiding. There were two sons. Two! And what about my –

M1 + M2: Don't mention him again, please. (*Pause.*)

S: My father.

M1 + M2: Don't.

S: What was his name?

M1 + M2: **Stop this right now**, Isaac! (*Hold.*)

S: Father what's-his-name?

M1: I'm switching off.

S: He had two sons.

M2: I'm switching off.

S: Why are you changing the – ?

M1 + M2: Switch.

> *Lights dim suddenly on* **M1 + M2**, *now only faintly visible.*

S: __(M1)__ ? __(M2)__ ? (*Pause.*) Mother? Mom? Mama?
Maaamaaa… Hello. Hello? Are you avoid – ? Are
you there?

M1*'s voice*: Switch.

> *M1 stands, crosses to the centre, and exits via*
> *AZ's end, i.e. along the stage or ramp through*
> *the audience.*

S (*calling after* **M1** *and straining to see her in the*
dim light): Mom? Mother. __(M1)__ .

M2*'s voice*: Switch.

> *M2 stands, crosses to the centre, and also exits*
> *via* **AZ**'s *end.*

S (*calling after* **M2** *and straining to see her*): __(M2)__ .
Mother. Mom? Can you do that, leave me? With
nothing. Mom? Are you still there? I'll say I'm
sorry. For the record even, whatever that means, if
you want. Is this a… test? (*His last word echoes:*
"*…test…test…test…*") __(M1)__ ? __(M2)__ ? Mom./
Stop this right now, please, for the record – !

M1 + M2 + AZ*'s voices*: <u>Stop this right now, please,</u>
<u>for the record – </u>!

S: God, I sound exactly like them, exactly like…
(*Project and hold* **FATHER ABRAHAM**.)

M1 + M2's *voices*: Switch. (*House lights briefly up on the audience.*)

S: Hey... (*With some initial strain he notices the audience. House lights down.*) Hey... you've been watching, haven't you been watching me fill the boy only to kill what father of the man's in me, a void abandoned and bound bare as a sheet where father made mother lay us down, (*replace ABRAHAM with LAIUS to produce FATHER LAIUS*) father lay us and tied me with your guilty gaze to this hilltop, waiting among a captured flock, but you don't weep, you don't even try, and leave me for what, unadopted, just another black sheep crying blah blah baby have you any will? No sir, maaaam because our bond fates only one exit, doesn't it, across. (*Indicates AZ's end of the stage, where M1 + M2 exited.*) From the moment I arrived you must have had me nailed to the horizon with your eyes on my vanishing pointless boy you're all – mother, brother, father to yourself – all, then baited, mastered, cut off and switched for a bloody circumcised record.

M1 + M2's *voices*: Switch. (*House lights briefly up again, then down.*)

S: Yeah, I'm beginning to see... how your eyes have made me the prized **blind** sacrifice, a clueless anonymous offering, the onus among us. (*Hold.*) Or the **asshole**. (*Add.*) Well I surrender. That's all I can give now that you shepherded me to the end so you'll leave satisfied that you've won and I'm **nothing without others**. Thanks. I mean that. I needed this tacit deal we cut, our own little covenant.

*He stands and – with his ankles residually bruised from the Prelude – begins walking towards **AZ**'s former spot. He is now past his own microphone, speaking acoustically.*

I'm going to take the only way out. Feel free to stay or leave. You can even join my parents if you want. Seriously, feel free. (*Something stops him suddenly. He turns around and discovers that, under his shirt, he's attached to the chair by a strap tied around his waist.*) **Come on.**

He takes off his shirt, drops it on stage, and starts worming his way out of the strap, raising it above his shoulders. When the strap reaches his neck it inadvertently tightens.

Shit. (*He jams his fingers under the accidental noose to keep it from strangling him.*) This doesn't have to be a tragedy. It could just happen, maybe even off in some forest where nobody goes. But then we can't help but follow the story, can we, watching, reading, spewing and eating our own tales in the headlines because we are the record. **You are the record.** (*Hold.*) Remember that, will you? (*Add FORGET.*) Hypocrites, my brothers my sisters: clear cut or stumped I would have done the same in your shoes and not acted at all, sitting asses to asses, bust to bust.

> *He manages to slip the noose off his head. He looks up at the projection and* **YOU ARE THE RECORD** *fades out, leaving only* **FORGET**. *Then he limps back to his chair and starts wrapping the strap around the chair's 'torso' during the following song.*

M1/M2*'s voices (singing to the tune of 'Father Abraham'):*
Father what's-his-name,
Had two son sons.
And/But two son sons,
Had father what's-his-name.

S (*into his microphone*): Have you heard this one about Father? Join in the chorus if you want, or cover your ears. Either way, feel free. (*He wraps the end of the strap around the chair's 'neck'.*)

M1/M2*'s voices (singing):*
And/But they didn't laugh – yes/no!
And/But they didn't cry – yes/no!
All they did was go like this: switch.

> *Lights fade up on* **AZ**'s *microphone as* **S** *walks again towards it, stopping on his way to put his shirt back on, which now resembles the shirt* **AZ** *wore in Act I (see notes). The song repeats and on the next "switch" project and*

hold the photo of S's face from earlier. The
*held word, **FORGET**, is now contained in a*
horizontal black bar covering the eyes in the
photo. The singing ends.

AZ*'s voice*: For the record,/ have you seen this one
of my son?

S (*speaking into* **AZ***'s former microphone*): <u>Have</u>
<u>you seen this one of my son</u>? Remember it if you
want, or cover your eyes. Either way, feel free, feel
free.

AZ*'s voice*: God forbid.

M1 + M2*'s voices*: God bless.

We now hear two prayers chanted
simultaneously:

*Hebrew recording, emanating from **M1***'s side*
of the stage: "Baruch ata Hashem Eloheinu
melech ha'olam asher kidshanu bemitzvotav
vetzivanu lehachniso bebrito shel Avraham
Avinu."
*Arabic recording, emanating from **M2***'s side*:
"Allahu Akbar, Allahu Akbar."
*During this recitation fade out **FORGET**,*
leaving S's photo with a wordless black bar
covering the eyes. S exits.

M1 + M2*'s voices*: Switch.

Lights fade out, except for the strap wrapped around S's chair, which begins to glow. The projection of S's 'censored' face cross-fades into a photo of AZ's face blindfolded (similar to the photo of AZ's masked face in the beginning of Act I).

Hebrew recording (from M2's side): "Baruch ata Hashem..."
Arabic recording (from M1's side): "Allahu Akbar, Allahu Akbar."

Prayers end.

M1 + M2's *voices*: Switch.

Blackout.

The chairs and the horse may be made of wood.

The reins on **AZ**'s horse and the strap attached to **S**'s chair may match.

In Act II, **S** wears a reversible shirt with two different patterns. When taking off the shirt near the end of the play, he pulls it inside out, revealing a pattern that matches **AZ**'s shirt from Act I. In this way, he puts on "**AZ**'s shirt" before his final exit.

The first word of Genesis, which is the Hebrew word for "in the beginning" – בראשית – has been transliterated as "bare sheet."

In addition to being the Muslim call to prayer, the *adhan* ("God is great…") is the first prayer recited to a newborn after delivery. The Hebrew prayer is part of the Jewish circumcision ceremony, and translates as: "Blessed are you, The Name, our god, king of the universe, who has sanctified us with his commandments, and has commanded us to bring him into the covenant of Abraham, our forefather."

This is a score – to play.

ABOUT THE AUTHOR

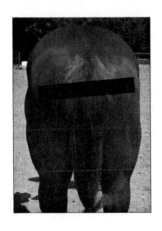

ADAM SEELIG is a poet, playwright, stage director, and the founder of One Little Goat Theatre Company in Toronto, with which he has premiered works by Yehuda Amichai, Thomas Bernhard, Jon Fosse and himself. Born and raised in Vancouver, Seelig has also lived in Northern California, New York and Jerusalem. His previous plays include *All Is Almost Still* (New York 2004) and *Antigone : Insurgency* (Toronto 2007). He is the recipient of a Commonwealth Fellowship and a Stanford Golden Grant for his work on Samuel Beckett's manuscripts, and his writings appear in various publications, including *World Literature Today*, *Modern Drama*, *BafterC*, *jwcurry #381* and *Poetry Magazine*.

COLOPHON

Manufactured in an edition of 400 copies by BookThug in conjunction with One Little Goat Theatre Company's premiere of *Talking Masks* at the Walmer Centre Theatre, November 13 - 28, 2009 in Toronto.

WWW.BOOKTHUG.CA

BOOK
PRODUCTION
WAR ECONOMY
STANDARD

Book design by Jay MillAr
Cover image by Adam Seelig
Printed in Canada